Martino Fine Books, Eastford CT, 2021

Martino Fine Books
P.O. Box 913,
Eastford, CT 06242 USA

ISBN   978-1-68422-529-3

Copyright 2021
Martino Fine Books

Cover Design Tiziana Matarazzo

Printed in the United States of America On 100% Acid-Free Paper

IN MONTGOMERY, ALABAMA, 50,000 NEGROES FOUND A NEW WAY TO WORK FOR FREEDOM, *WITHOUT VIOLENCE AND WITHOUT HATING.* BECAUSE THEY DID, THEY PUT NEW HOPE IN ALL MEN WHO SEEK BROTHERHOOD, AND WHO KNOW YOU DON'T BUILD IT WITH BULLETS. NO ONE PERSON MADE THE MONTGOMERY STORY, BUT ONE MAN'S NAME STOOD OUT AMONG THE HUNDREDS WHO WORKED SO HARD AND UNSELFISHLY. THAT MAN WAS 29-YEAR-OLD MARTIN LUTHER KING, JR., MINISTER OF THE DEXTER AVENUE BAPTIST CHURCH AND PRESIDENT OF THE MONTGOMERY IMPROVEMENT ASSOCIATION.

YOUNG MARTIN GREW UP IN THE SHADOW OF T CHURCH. HIS FATHER WAS PASTOR OF ONE OF T LARGEST BAPTIST CHURCHES IN ATLANTA, WHE MARTIN WAS BORN.

THE BASIC BOOK IN THE KING HOUSE WAS THE BIBLE. FROM IT YOUNG MARTIN EARLY LEARNED JESUS' TEACHINGS ABOUT *LOVE* AND ITS POWER.

... AND LOVE THY NEIGHBOR AS THYSELF.

HOLY BIBLE

MARTIN FINISHED HIGH SCHOOL AT 15 AND ENTERED MOREHOUSE COLLEGE IN ATLANTA. THERE HE WORKED WITH THE CITY'S INTERCOLLEGIATE CHRISTIAN COUNCIL, WITH BOTH WHITE AND COLORED STUDENTS.

SOME OF *US* DON'T LIKE DISCRIMINATION, EITHER, MARTIN.

AT CROZER SEMINARY, ONE OF SIX NEGROES AMONG NEARLY 100 STUDENTS, HE WAS ELECTED PRESIDENT OF THE STUDENT BODY AND GRADUATED AT THE HEAD OF HIS CLASS...

WHERE TO NOW, MARTIN?

TO BOSTON, FOR MORE STUDY. I NEED TO KNOW MORE BEFORE I START PREACHING.

WHILE HE STUDIED FOR A PH.D. DEGREE AT BOSTON UNIVERSITY, HE MET AND MARRIED CORETTA SCOTT, A PRETTY YOUNG SINGER.

I NEVER THOUGHT I'D MARRY A PREACHER.

I'M GLAD YOU CHANGED YOUR MIND.

NORTHERN CHURCHES WERE OPEN TO THE YOU MINISTER, BUT IN 1954, M TIN LUTHER KING AND BRIDE DECIDED TO RETU TO THE SOUTH.

IT'S HEF THAT GO WANTS ME BE, I KNO

ONE YEAR LATER, MONTGOMERY, ALABAMA...

I'M A PEACEFUL MAN--BUT I HAVE A GUN. FOR A LONG TIME I THOUGHT I MIGHT HAVE TO USE IT SOME DAY. NOW I DON'T KNOW...

CALL ME JONES. MY NAME DOESN'T MATTER. BUT MY STORY'S IMPORTANT FOR YOU AS WELL AS ME. WE'RE ALL CAUGHT UP IN IT IN ONE WAY OR ANOTHER!

LIVE IN MONTGOMERY, ALABAMA. I LOVE MONTGOMERY, BUT I'VE HATED IT, TOO. A NEGRO ANYWHERE IN THE DEEP SOUTH HAS A HARD TIME. JIM CROW SITS MIGHTY HEAVY ON A MAN'S SPIRIT.

PEOPLE LIVE SCARED UNDER JIM CROW. I WAS SCARED, TOO. YOU NEVER KNOW WHEN SOMETHING MIGHT BUST OUT, AND I HAVE A WIFE AND BABY.

SNAP IT UP, BOY. I WANT THAT CAR IN A HURRY.

SAY HELLO TO DADDY...

DA...

NOW TAKE ROSA PARKS. SHE REALLY HAD COURAGE. SAT THERE IN THE BUS THAT NIGHT AND JUST QUIETLY SAID NO WHEN THE BUS DRIVER TOLD HER TO GIVE HER SEAT TO A WHITE MAN.

AND HOW'S MY LITTLE BOY TODAY?

DA!

FOR THE LAST TIME... ARE YOU GETTING UP... OR AREN'T YOU?

WE USED TO PLAY--THE BABY AND I--RIGHT NEXT TO THE BUREAU WITH THAT LOADED GUN. I WONDERED IF I'D HAVE THE COURAGE TO USE IT TO DEFEND MY FAMILY. LATELY I'VE STARTED TO WONDER IF THAT REALLY WOULD BE COURAGE.

BECAUSE SHE WAS TIRED AND HER FEET ACHED, ROSA PARKS **REFUSED** TO GIVE UP HER SEAT IN THE BUS. ROSA PARKS WAS ARRESTED.

THAT NIGHT I COULDN'T SLEEP. I WAS GETTING SICK AND TIRED OF ALL THIS. I WOKE UP MY WIFE.

SOMETHING OUGHT TO BE DONE. ROSA IS A GOOD WOMAN AND NOT A TROUBLE MAKER. THEY HAD NO RIGHT ARRESTING HER!

BUT WHAT CAN WE DO?

I DECIDED TO TALK TO SOME OF MY FRIENDS, THE VERY NEXT DAY...

THEY MAKE US MOVE IF ANY WHITE PERSON WANTS OUR SEAT. WE OUGHT TO **PROTEST**-- AND NOT RIDE THE BUSES FOR A DAY.

NOW HERE'S MY PLAN...

WE GOT OUT A MIMEOGRAPHED SHEET PROTESTING WHAT HAD HAPPENED TO ROSA PARKS AND CALLING FOR A ONE-DAY BOYCOTT OF THE BUSES.

THERE ARE 50,000 NEGROES IN MONTGOMERY-- HOW MANY OF THEM CAN WE REACH WITH JUST A **FEW HUNDRED COPIES** OF THIS LEAFLET?

LET'S JUST HOPE THAT THOSE WHO REAL IT SPREA THE WORD

THAT NIGHT, WORD WAS FLASHED AROUND TOWN THAT THE PROTEST WAS SET FOR THE NEXT DAY.

YOU HEAR THE NEWS?

SURE DID. **NOBODY'S** GOING TO RIDE THE BUSES TOMORROW.

THE NEWSPAPERS OF MONTGOMERY HELPE MORE THAN THEY KNEW.

LOOK AT THIS! THEY'VE PRINTED IT UP BIG FOR EVERYONE TO READ.

THAT'S WON DERFUL. WE COULDN'T HAVE REACHED THAT MANY PEOPLE WIT **OUR** LITTLE SHEET. NOW EVERYONE WILL KNOW WHAT TO DO.

NEGROES PLAN BUS BOYCOTT

DECEMBER 5, 1955 -- THE DAY OF THE PROTEST, EVERYONE WALKED...

...OR RODE IN A FRIEND'S CAR... OR HITCHED A RIDE WITH NEGRO TAXI DRIVERS.

OUR PROTEST IS A SUCCESS! NO ONE'S RIDING THOSE BUSES.

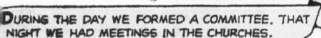

DURING THE DAY WE FORMED A COMMITTEE. THAT NIGHT WE HAD MEETINGS IN THE CHURCHES.

WE'RE CALLING OURSELVES THE MONTGOMERY IMPROVEMENT ASSOCIATION. WE'RE GOING TO SEE TO IT THAT NEGROES ARE TREATED *FAIRLY* IN THE BUSES OF MONTGOMERY...

THE CROWDS WERE HUGE. WE USED LOUDSPEAKERS SO THAT THOSE WHO COULDN'T GET IN COULD HEAR WHAT WAS HAPPENING FROM OUT ON THE STREETS...

... I WANT YOU TO MEET THE LEADER WE HAVE CHOSEN TODAY... REVEREND *MARTIN LUTHER KING, JR.!*

THAT TIME I KNEW MARTIN LUTHER KING [ON]LY SLIGHTLY, BUT I SOON LEARNED THAT A [NE]W AND IMPORTANT LEADER HAD COME ON [TH]E SCENE -- ONE AMERICA WOULD FEEL PROUD

YOU ALL KNOW OF THE SUCCESS OF OUR ONE-DAY PROTEST. BUT A SINGLE DAY IS NOT ENOUGH. LET'S *STAY* OFF THE BUSES UNTIL WE CAN RIDE THEM WITH DIGNITY. LET'S WALK TO FREEDOM.'

THIS IS A *NONVIOLENT* PROTEST AGAINST INJUSTICE. OUR CHIEF WEAPONS ARE MORAL AND SPIRITUAL FORCES. WE DEPEND ON LOVE! LOVE AND GOODWILL TOWARD *ALL* MEN MUST BE AT THE FOREFRONT OF OUR MOVEMENT IF IT IS TO BE SUCCESSFUL.

AND SO BEGAN THE **WALK TO FREEDOM.** DURING THE DAY WE WALKED... AT NIGHT WE HELD PRAYER MEETINGS.

ARE WE GOING TO RIDE THOSE BUSES?

NO!

ARE WE GOING TO WALK WITH THE FEET GOD GAVE US?

YES!

YES! BETTER TO WALK WITH DIGNITY...THAN RIDE IN HUMILIATION!

WE WALKED AND WALKED AND WALKED...AND SOMETIMES THUMBED A RIDE LIKE ANY HITCH-HIKER.

ROOM FOR EVERYBODY! STEP RIGHT IN-- THERE'S NO CHARGE!

THAT'S JUST GREAT! OTHERWISE I HAVE TO WALK FOUR MILES TO WORK.

THINGS WERE GOING ALMOST TOO GOOD. T[H] WAS BOUND TO BE TROUBLE.

YOU FAILED TO SIGNAL FOR A TURN.

BUT I DI[D] TURN AT ALL! I'VE B[EEN] DRIVING STRAIGHT DOW[N] THE ROAD FOR MORE THAN [A] MILE[S]

TELL IT TO THE JUDGE. I'M GIVING YOU A TICKET.

THE POLICE OFFICERS KEPT BOTHERING US. THEY EVEN STOPPED MARTIN LUTHER KING'S CAR.

WHAT'S THE CHARGE, OFFICER?

30 MILES IN A 25 MILE ZONE. WHY DON'T YOU PEOPLE GET WISE TO YOURSELVES AND GIVE UP THIS BOYCOTT?

WE WEREN'T GOING TO GIVE UP! WE DECIDED TO BUY STATION WAGONS WITH CONTRIBUTIONS SENT IN BY WHITE AND NEGRO SYMPATHIZERS ALL OVER THE COUNTRY.

D. J. SIMMS AND RUFUS LEWIS LAID[?] OUT THE ROUTES A[ND] PICK-UP POINTS. BEFORE WE REALI[ZED] IT, WE HAD A TRA[NS]PORTATION SYSTE[M] OF OUR OWN.

JANUARY 30, 1956. SOMETHING HAPPENED ON THAT DAY THAT TOUCHED MY HEART AND DID SOMETHING TO ME. MARTIN LUTHER KING WAS SPEAKING AT A MEETING...

THIS IS A SPIRITUAL MOVEMENT...VIOLENCE WILL DEFEAT OUR PURPOSE. VIOLENCE IS NOT ONLY IMPRACTICAL BUT IMMORAL.

MRS. KING WAS AT HOME TALKING TO A FRIEND...

CORETTA--DID YOU HEAR THAT? SOUNDED LIKE SOMEONE THREW A BRICK!

WHY DON'T WE MOVE INTO THE BACK ROOM WHERE WE CAN TALK IN PEACE?

SUDDENLY...

BOOM!

REVEREND KING! FIRST THING I WANT YOU TO KNOW IS THAT CORETTA AND THE BABY ARE ALL RIGHT. THEN I'VE GOT TO TELL YOU THEY'VE JUST EXPLODED A BOMB IN YOUR HOME!

MARTIN LUTHER KING RUSHED HOME. A CROWD WAS GATHERED OUTSIDE. THEY WERE IN AN ANGRY MOOD, WANTING TO ANSWER VIOLENCE WITH VIOLENCE. AND THEN KING SPOKE TO THEM.

PLEASE BE PEACEFUL. WE BELIEVE IN LAW AND ORDER. WE ARE NOT ADVOCATING VIOLENCE. I WANT YOU TO LOVE OUR ENEMIES...FOR WHAT WE ARE DOING IS RIGHT. WHAT WE ARE DOING IS JUST-- AND GOD IS WITH US.

LATER, WE WALKED BACK THROUGH THE NIGHT TO OUR HOMES...

IF A MAN CAN SEE HIS HOME BOMBED AND NOT FIGHT BACK--EXCEPT WITH LOVE-- THEN THERE IS HOPE FOR ALL OF US.

THOUGH WE TRIED TO LOVE OUR ENEMIES, THEIR HEARTS WERE NOT SOFTENED TOWARD US. IN THEIR ATTEMPT TO BREAK UP OUR BUS PROTEST, THEY INDICTED 93 OF OUR LEADERS, INCLUDING E. D. NIXON, OF THE SLEEPING CAR PORTERS UNION.

LOOKING FOR ME? WELL, HERE I AM.

WE WERE THRILLED TO SEE MANY OF OUR LEADERS SURRENDER WITHOUT BEING HUNTE[DOWN...

THOSE ARRESTS WERE LAST MINUTE DESPERATION MEASURES ON THE PART OF THOSE WHO KNEW THAT SOME DAY SOON, RIGHT AND JUSTICE WOULD PREVAIL. AS REVEREND RALPH ABERNATHY SAID...

AT THIS MOMENT, THE SUPREME COURT IS CONSIDERING OUR CASE AGAINST THE BUS COMPANY. ONE DAY SOON WE ARE GOING BACK TO THE BUSES. WE MUST GET READY FOR THAT DAY.

WE BEGAN TO MAKE PREPARATIONS FOR WHAT WE WOULD DO WHEN WE GOT BACK ON THE BUSES. THINGS WOULD BE DIFFERENT. WE ACTED IT ALL OUT.

NOW, I'M THE BUS DRIVER, AND CATHERINE HERE IS COMING ABOARD TO PAY HER FARE. AND SHE'S COMING IN THROUGH THE FRONT DOOR!

MOVE ALONG, THERE! GET TO THE BACK OF THE BUS!

THANK YOU, MR. BUS DRIVER, BUT THE BACK IS CROWDED. I THINK I'LL TAKE THIS EMPTY SEAT HERE.

WELL, YOU'RE SUPPOSED TO GO TO THE BACK.

ARGUING WON'T HELP. I'LL JUST SIT QUIET.

THAT WAS HOW WE GOT READY TO GO BACK ON THE BUSES. TO MAKE SURE WE WOULD NOT BE ACCUSED OF VIOLENCE, WE DECIDED TO CLASP OUR HANDS IN OUR LAPS AND NOT US[THEM AGAINS[ANYONE, NO MATTE[WHAT HAPPENED[

THEN I SAW A NEWS DISPATCH THAT MADE MY HEART JUMP...

THE U.S. SUPREME COURT HAS DECLARED BUS SEGREGATION *ILLEGAL* IN MONTGOMERY!

DAILY COURIER SUPREME COURT RULES BUS SEGREGATION ILLEGAL IN MONTGOMERY

ON DECEMBER 21, WE WENT BACK ON THE BUSES. SOMEONE SHOUTED VILE AND ABUSIVE WORDS AT A YOUNG FELLOW WHO WAS GETTING ON THE BUS.

ONCE I WOULD HAVE GOTTEN SORE ABOUT THAT-- AND SHOUTED DIRTY WORDS BACK--AND MAYBE HIT BACK!

BUT NOW IT WAS DIFFERENT FOR ALL OF US. WE ALL JUST *SMILED*. AND THAT DID SOMETHING TO THE MAN WHO SHOUTED. THE NEWSPAPER FELLOWS TOOK HIS PICTURE...

HEY! YOU'RE SMILING! I THOUGHT YOU WERE MAD AT THESE PEOPLE!

I AM! BUT IT'S PRETTY HARD TO *STAY* MAD WHEN THEY DON'T FIGHT BACK!

ONE BUS DRIVER MADE A WOMAN PAY HER FARE TWICE.

I'M GOING TO PRAY FOR YOU.

HERE! TAKE BACK YOUR FARE-- I DON'T WANT *YOU* PRAYING FOR *ME*!

ON ANOTHER BUS, SOMEONE SLAPPED A WOMAN.

I COULD REALLY WALLOP HIM-- HE'S SMALLER THAN ME! BUT I'M GOING TO REMEMBER WHAT REVEREND KING TOLD ME ABOUT PEACE AND NON-VIOLENCE. I'LL JUST KEEP MY HANDS CLASPED. THAT WAY THERE WON'T BE ANY TROUBLE.

AT FIRST, A FEW BUSES ON NIGHT RUNS WERE PEPPERED WITH SHOTGUN BLASTS.

CRASH!

THEN THINGS SEEMED TO QUIET DOWN. IT WAS A FALSE QUIET.

THEN THE NIGHT BOMBINGS BEGAN. THERE WERE SEVEN OF THEM.

ONE OF THE HOMES BOMBED WAS THAT OF REVER... ROBERT GRAETZ, WHITE PASTOR OF A NEGRO LUTHE... CHURCH, WHO HAD BEEN ONE OF US RIGHT FROM T... START.

I AM PLANTING A TREE IN THI... BOMB CRATER TO REMIND US TH... IN THE MIDST OF DEATH, THER... IS *LIFE*... AND HOPE.

NEGRO CHURCHES WERE BOMBED AND AN UNEX- PLODED BOMB WAS FOUND ON KING'S FRONT PORCH. BUT NOW MONTGOMERY'S LAW-ABIDING WHITE CITIZENS TURNED AGAINST THE VIOLENCE.

IT'S GOT TO STOP. THESE BOMBINGS ARE GIVING MONTGOMERY A BAD NAME.

I AGREE. THE BUS FIGHT IS OVER ANYWAY. IT'S THE LAW OF THE LAND.

IF WHAT HAPPENED HERE IS A VICTORY... ANYONE AT ALL, IT'S FOR ALL MONTGOME... WE RESPECT OURSELVES MORE AND WE K... THAT THE IDEA OF LOVE AND NON-VIOLENC... SPREADING. I'VE *THROWN MY GUN AWA...* IT HAD GOTTEN MUCH TOO HEAVY FOR M... EVER TO LIFT AGAIN!

BUS STOP

MARTIN LUTHER KING TELLS
HOW A NATION WON ITS FREEDOM BY THE MONTGOMERY METHOD

YEARS BEFORE OUR WALK TO FREEDOM, A COUNTRY OF 300,000,000 PEOPLE WON ITS *INDEPENDENCE* BY THE SAME METHODS WE USED...

"MAHATMA GANDHI STARTED HIS CAMPAIGN FOR FREEDOM IN INDIA IN 1919. IT LOOKED HOPELESS. THE BRITISH EMPIRE WAS THE *STRONGEST* THE WORLD HAD EVER KNOWN. INDIA'S PEOPLE WERE POOR AND POWERLESS."

"THE NEW CAMPAIGN MEANT *SUFFERING* AND EVEN DEATH. WHEN GANDHI CALLED ON THE PEOPLE TO FAST AND PRAY TO PROTEST A BAD LAW, THE BRITISH SHOT DOWN HUNDREDS OF THEM AT AMRITSAR. IT RAISED HORRIFIED PROTESTS ALL OVER THE WORLD."

"...AGAIN AND AGAIN THEY PUT GANDHI IN PRISON, BUT THAT DID NOT STOP HIM. HE WOULD WAIT PATIENTLY, THINKING AND PRAYING, AND AS *SOON* AS HE WAS OUT WOULD START AGAIN..."

"MILLIONS OF THE POORER PEOPLE IN INDIA WERE CALLED *'UNTOUCHABLES'.* THEY COULD NOT EVEN USE THE PUBLIC HIGHWAY. GANDHI RENAMED THEM 'HARIJAN--CHILDREN OF GOD,' AND LED THEM TO STAND IN THE FORBIDDEN ROAD. IT TOOK 16 MONTHS OF STANDING, BUT THEN THE POLICE GAVE IN AND LET THEM PASS."

"THE BRITISH PUT A TAX ON SALT, AND SAID INDIANS COULD NOT MAKE THEIR OWN SALT. GANDHI *WALKED* WITH HIS FOLLOWERS 200 MILES TO THE SEA TO BREAK THE LAW BY GATHERING SALT. SOON THE JAILS WERE OVERFLOWING WITH INDIANS-- AND THE BRITISH DID AWAY WITH THE SALT ACT."

"IT BECAME HARDER AND HARDER FOR THE BRITISH TO KEEP CONTROL. THEIR *JAILS WERE FILLED* WITH INDIA'S BEST-LOVED LEADERS, INCLUDING SUCH MEN AS NEHRU, WHO LATER BECAME PRIME MINISTER."

"BESIDES, THE NEWS THAT BRITISH SOLDIERS WERE SHOOTING UNARMED MEN AND WOMEN AND PUTTING LEADERS IN JAIL, WAS TROUBLING THE BRITISH AT HOME."

THE VOTERS IN MY DISTRICT DON'T LIKE WHAT WE'RE DOING IN INDIA.

WE'LL HAVE TO GET OUT. THAT'S CLEAR.

"...FINALLY THE BRITISH GAVE IN AND GRANTED INDIA'S *INDEPENDENCE*. GANDHI HAD MADE A REVOLUTION WITHOUT FIRING A SHOT."

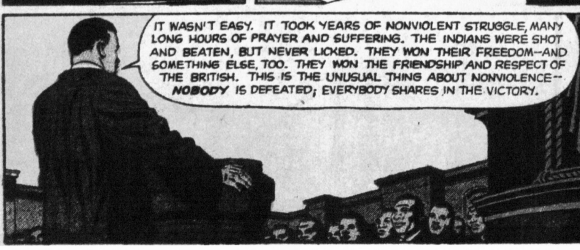

IT WASN'T EASY. IT TOOK YEARS OF NONVIOLENT STRUGGLE, MANY LONG HOURS OF PRAYER AND SUFFERING. THE INDIANS WERE SHOT AND BEATEN, BUT NEVER LICKED. THEY WON THEIR FREEDOM--AND SOMETHING ELSE, TOO. THEY WON THE FRIENDSHIP AND RESPECT OF THE BRITISH. THIS IS THE UNUSUAL THING ABOUT NONVIOLENCE-- *NOBODY* IS DEFEATED; EVERYBODY SHARES IN THE VICTORY.

HOW THE MONTGOMERY METHOD WORKS

IN MONTGOMERY WE USED THIS NONVIOLENT CHRISTIAN ACTION TO GET JIM CROW OFF THE BUSES. IT CAN BE USED ANYWHERE, THOUGH, AGAINST ANY KIND OF EVIL. HERE IS HOW IT WORKS.

FIRST, REMEMBER THAT *YOU* CAN DO SOMETHING ABOUT THE SITUATION, NOT JUST THE GOVERNMENT, OR SOME BIG ORGANIZATION, BUT *YOU*. GOD SAYS *YOU* ARE IMPORTANT. HE NEEDS *YOU* TO CHANGE THINGS.

THE SECOND THING IS MUCH HARDER. GOD LOVES YOUR *ENEMY*, TOO, AND THAT MAKES *HIM* IMPORTANT TO YOU. YOU HAVE TO SEE *HIM* AS A HUMAN BEING, LIKE YOURSELF. YOU HAVE TO TRY TO *UNDERSTAND* HIM AND *SYMPATHIZE* WITH HIM.

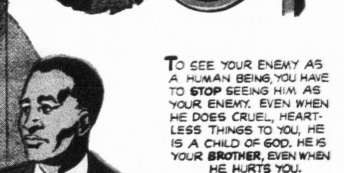

TO SEE YOUR ENEMY AS A HUMAN BEING, YOU HAVE TO *STOP* SEEING HIM AS YOUR ENEMY. EVEN WHEN HE DOES CRUEL, HEARTLESS THINGS TO YOU, HE IS A CHILD OF GOD. HE IS YOUR *BROTHER*, EVEN WHEN HE HURTS YOU.

WHITES ONLY

HARDEST OF ALL, YOU HAVE TO HELP YOUR ENEMY TO SEE **YOU** AS A HUMAN BEING. HE HAS TO SEE YOU AS A PERSON WHO WANTS THE **SAME KIND** OF THINGS HE WANTS: LOVE, A FAMILY, A JOB, THE RESPECT OF HIS NEIGHBORS.

IT WILL BE EASIER FOR HIM TO SEE YOU THIS W[AY] IF YOU ACT LIKE A BROTHER. SO, EVEN WHEN [HE] TRIES TO HURT YOU, YOU MUST NOT STRIKE BA[CK] EVEN IN YOUR THOUGHTS, YOU MUST NOT STRI[KE] BACK. YOU MUST GO ON **LOVING** HIM. LIKE [THE] SCHOOLGIRL IN LITTLE ROCK, YOU MUST SAY, "FATHER, FORGIVE THEM, FOR THEY KNOW NOT WHAT THEY DO."

THIS DOES NOT MEAN GIVING UP, THOUGH. IT IS **WRONG** FOR THIS BROTHER OF YOURS TO TREAT YOU AS THOUGH YOU WERE NOT A HUMAN BEING, AND IT WOULD BE **WRONG** FOR YOU TO HELP HIM TREAT YOU THIS WAY. YOU HAVE TO DO SOMETHING TO STOP HIM.

HE IS A HUMAN BEING AND SO HE CAN TRE[AT] YOU BADLY ONLY BECAUSE, SOMEHOW, HE IS **AFRAID** OF YOU, OR OF WHAT YOU MIGHT [DO] TO HIM. IF YOU TRY TO STOP HIM BY USIN[G] VIOLENCE AND BY "GETTING EVEN", HE WI[LL] BE SURE HE IS RIGHT IN BEING AFRAID OF Y[OU]

IF YOU SHOW HIM LOVE, THOUGH, YOU START TO TAKE AWAY THE REASON FOR HIS FEAR AND YOU MAKE IT **HARDER** FOR HIM TO GO ON HATING YOU. HERE'S **HOW TO GO** ABOUT IT.

First, DECIDE WHAT SPECIAL THING YOU'RE GOING TO WORK ON. IN MONTGOMERY, IT WAS BUSES, SOMEWHERE ELSE IT MIGHT BE *VOTING*, OR *SCHOOLS*, OR *INTEGRATED CHURCHES*. DON'T TRY TO DEAL WITH EVERYTHING WRONG AT ONCE.

Second, BE SURE YOU KNOW THE FACTS ABOUT THE SITUATION. DON'T ACT ON THE BASIS OF RUMORS OR HALF-TRUTHS. FIND OUT.

Third, WHERE YOU CAN, *TALK* TO THE PEOPLE CONCERNED. TRY TO EXPLAIN HOW YOU FEEL, AND WHY YOU FEEL AS YOU DO. *DON'T ARGUE*—JUST TELL THEM YOUR SIDE, AND LISTEN TO THEIRS. SOMETIMES YOU'LL BE SURPRISED TO FIND *FRIENDS* AMONG THOSE YOU THOUGHT WERE ENEMIES.

[NE]XT, BE SURE YOU ARE READY. *JOIN* [WIT]H OTHERS WHO FEEL THE WAY YOU DO. [HA]VE SOMEONE WITH EXPERIENCE COME IN [AND] TELL YOU HOW TO GET READY. TRY [PR]*ACTICE* SITUATIONS AS WE DID IN [MO]NTGOMERY. MAKE SURE [YO]U CAN FACE ANY OPPOSI-[TIO]N *WITHOUT HITTING* [B]*ACK, OR RUNNING AWAY, OR HATING.*

When YOU ARE READY, THEN GO AHEAD, AND *DON'T TURN BACK* NO MATTER HOW HARD THE WAY OR HOW LONG THE STRUGGLE. WHEN MY FRIEND, THE REV. RALPH ABERNATHY, FOUND HIMSELF ABOUT TO BE PUT IN JAIL IN MONTGOMERY, HE PRAYED, "GOD, I'M *AFRAID* TO GO TO JAIL. I'VE NEVER BEEN IN JAIL BEFORE. IF I GO, GOD, WILL YOU GO WITH ME?"